BOXER
FUN IS OUR BUSINESS

www.booksbyboxer.com

Bee Three Books

Bee Three Publishing is an imprint of Books By Boxer
Published by
Books By Boxer, Leeds, LS13 4BS, UK
Books by Boxer (EU), Dublin, D02 P593, IRELAND
Boxer Gifts LLC, 955 Sawtooth Oak Cir, VA 22802, USA

cs@boxer.gifts

Printed in Malta
ISBN: 9781917954372

MIX
Paper | Supporting responsible forestry
FSC® C022612
FSC www.fsc.org

This book is produced from responsibly sourced paper to ensure forest management

Stephen on Technology:

"This is the point. One technology doesn't replace another, it complements. Books are no more threatened by Kindle than stairs by elevators."

Stephen on Ideas:

"An original idea. That can't be too hard. The library must be full of them."

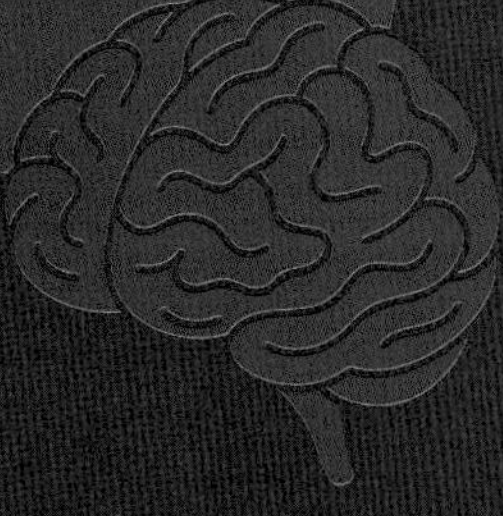

Stephen on His Nose:

"Over the years, however, my nose grew and grew, and it became apparent by the time I was fourteen that, like its owner, it was not growing straight."

- Moab Is My Washpot

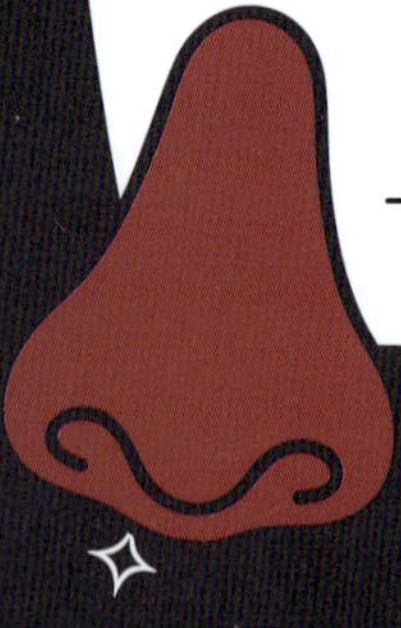

Stephen on Curiosity:

"The only reason people do not know much is because they do not care to know. They are incurious. Incuriosity is the oddest and most foolish failing there is."

- The Fry Chronicles

Stephen on Growth:

"Am I the same person I was fifty years ago? Every molecule and cell of my body has been replaced many times over."

- Heroes: Mortals and Monsters, Quests and Adventures

Stephen on His Values:

"I am a lover of truth, a worshipper of freedom, a celebrant at the altar of language and purity and tolerance."

Stephen on His Sexuality:

"My first words, as I was being born [...] I looked up at my mother and said, 'That's the last time I'm going up one of those.'"

Stephen on Adolescence:

"No adolescent ever wants to be understood, which is why they complain about being misunderstood all the time."

- Moab Is My Washpot

Stephen on the Finer Things in Life:

"It is the useless things that make life worth living and that make life dangerous too: wine, love, art, beauty. Without them, life is safe, but not worth bothering with."

- Moab Is My Washpot

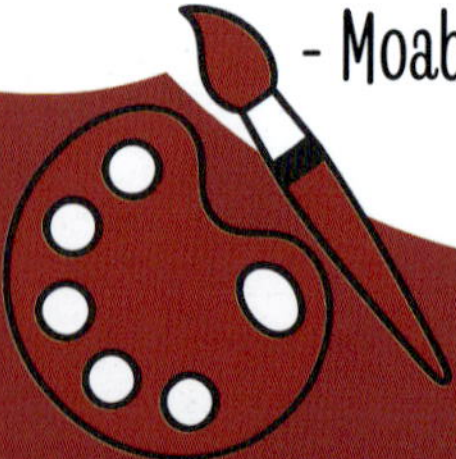

Stephen on Clichés:

"It is a cliché that most clichés are true, but then, like most clichés, that cliché is untrue."

Stephen on First Love:

"First love is unrequited ultimately because it's so huge. It's such an act of giving, and it requires so much back that it can never be given back. It's like an atom bomb. It's like... It's all the energy of who you are and who you want to be and what you love and what you hope to be, explodes. It is impossible for a single... human being to offer that back to you in a mutual way."

Stephen on His Common Sense:

"I always feel a fool when in the company of people who work for a living. It brings out my startling lack of common sense."

"Gaia visited her daughter Mnemosyne, who was busy being unpronounceable."

- Mythos: The Greek Myths Retold

Stephen on Reinvention:

"I like to wake up each morning and not know what I think, that I may reinvent myself in some way."

- The Independent, September 2004

Stephen on the Daily Mail:

"How can one not be fond of something that the Daily Mail despises?"

Stephen on Being Able to Change:

"People who can change and change again are so much more reliable and happier than those who can't."

- Moab Is My Washpot

"There were
people who believed their
opportunities to live a fulfilled life
were hampered by the number of Asians in
England, by the existance of a royal family, by
the volume of traffic that passed by their house,
by the malice of trade unions, by the power of
callous employers, by the refusal of the health
service to take their condition seriously, by
communism, by capitalism, by atheism, by
anything, in fact, but their own futile,
weak-minded failure to get a
f***ing grip."

- Revenge

Stephen on Rejection:

"How to separate the humiliation from the loss, that's the catch. You can never be sure if what tortures you is the pain of being without someone you love or the embarrassment of admitting that you have been rejected."

- Making History

Stephen on Swearing:

"The sort of twee person who thinks swearing is in any way a sign of a lack of education or a lack of verbal interest is just a f***ing lunatic."

"Better sexy and racy than sexist and racist."

Stephen on His Age:

"I don't need you to remind me of my age. I have a bladder to do that for me."

- Daily Telegraph circa 1990

Stephen on Compromise:

"Compromise is a stalling between two fools."

Stephen on His Power:

"I used many times to touch my own chest and feel, under its asthmatic quiver, the engine of the heart and lungs and blood, and feel amazed at what I sensed was the enormity of the power I possessed. Not magical power, but real power. The power simply to go on, the power to endure, that is power enough, but I felt I had also the power to create, to add, to delight, to amaze, and to transform."

- Moab Is My Washpot

Stephen on Enthusiasts:

"Enthusiasts are used to being mocked, maligned, and misunderstood. We don't really mind."

- The Fry Chronicles

Stephen on His Alarm:

"The alarm in the morning? Well, I have an old tape of Carlo Maria Giulini conducting the Vienna Philharmonic Orchestra in a perfectly transcendent version in Shubert's seventh symphony. And I've rigged it up so that at exactly 7:30 every morning it falls from the ceiling onto my face."

Stephen on the Power of Words:

"Sticks and stones may break my bones, but words will always hurt me. Bones mend and become actually stronger in the very place they were broken and where they have knitted up; mental wounds can grind and ooze for decades and be re-opened by the quietest whisper."

- Moab Is My Washpot

Stephen on the Good and the Bad:

"For the world seems never to offer anything worthwhile without also providing a dreadful opposite."

- Mythos: The Greek Myths Retold

Stephen on His Mind:

"I'm fat because I'm greedy, and if my mind is fat, it's because I'm curious."

Stephen on Honesty:

"A true thing, poorly expressed, becomes a lie."

Stephen on Intimacy:

"Sex without smiling is as sickly and as base as vodka and tonic without ice."

Stephen on Knowledge

"People sometimes accuse me of knowing a lot. 'Stephen,' they say, accusingly, 'you know a lot.' This is a bit like telling a person who has a few grains of sand clinging to him that he owns much sand. When you consider the vast amount of sand there is in the world such a person is, to all intents and purposes, sandless. We are all sandless. We are all ignorant. There are beaches and deserts and dunes of knowledge whose existance we have never even guessed at, let alone visited."

- The Book of General Ignorance

Stephen on Our Potential:

"We don't stop talking about how the world might be better just because we have no chance of making it to Prime Minister. We are all politicians. We are all artists. In an open society everything the mind and hands can achieve is our birthright. It is up to us to claim it."

- The Ode Less Travelled: Unlocking the Poet Within

Stephen on Words:

"If a thing can be said in ten words, I may be relied upon to take a hundred to say it. I ought to apologize for that. I ought to prune, pare, and extirpate excess growth, but I will not. I like words—strike that, I love words—and while I am fond of the condensed and economical use of them in poetry, in song lyrics, in Twitter, in good journalism and smart advertising, I love the luxuriant profusion and mad scatter of them too."

- The Fry Chronicles

Stephen on Good Advice:

"Gaia listened carefully to this wise counsel and—as we all do, whether mortal or immortal—ignored it."

- Mythos: The Greek Myths Retold

Stephen on Homophobia:

"The concept that really gets the goat of the gay-hater, the idea that really spins their melon and sickens their stomachs, is that most terrible and terrifying of all human notions, love.

That one can love another of the same gender, that is what the homophobe really cannot stand. Love in all eight tones and all five semitones of the world's full octave."

- Moab Is My Washpot

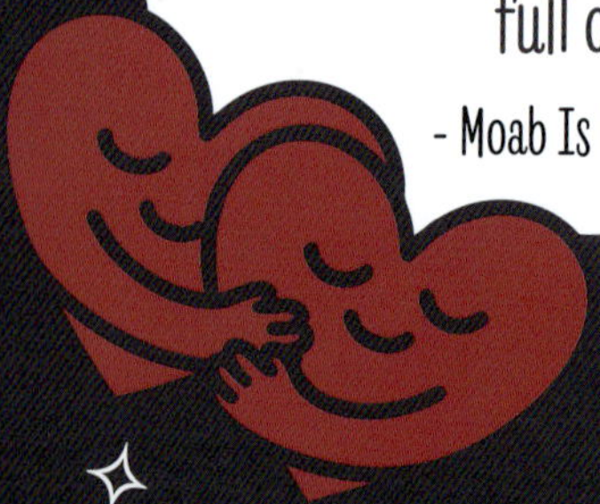

Stephen on Exploration:

"Taste every fruit of every tree in the garden at least once. It is an insult to creation not to experience it fully. Temperance is wickedness."

Stephen on Rulers:

"Those who rule the world get so little opportunity to run about and laugh and play in it."

- The Fry Chronicles

Stephen on His Musical Talents:

"I have Van Gogh's ear for music."

Stephen on Americans:

"We gave you a perfectly good language and you f***ed up."

Stephen on His Problems:

"As I go clowning my sentimental way into eternity, wrestling with all my problems of estrangement and communion, sincerity and simulation, ambition and acquiescence, I shuttle between worrying whether I matter at all and whether anything else matters but me."

- Moab Is My Washpot

Stephen on Pride:

"Part of life is learning what to be ashamed of and what to be proud of."

Stephen on Science:

"You'll often hear the phrase 'science doesn't know everything.' Well, of course it doesn't know everything. But just because science doesn't know everything doesn't mean that it knows nothing."

Stephen on Perspective:

"In a dung heap, even a plastic bead can gleam like a sapphire."

- The Hippopotamus

Stephen on life:

"Life, that can shower you with so much splendour, is unremittingly cruel to those who have given up."

- Moab Is My Washpot

Stephen on Progress:

"Progress isn't achieved by preachers or guardians of morality, but by madmen, hermits, heretics, dreamers, rebels, and sceptics."

Stephen on Money:

"Money is to Everything as an aeroplane is to Australia. The aeroplane isn't Australia, but it remains the only practical way we know of reaching it. So perhaps, metonymically, the aeroplane is Australia after all."

Stephen on Music:

"Music takes me to places of illimitable sensual and insensate joy, accessing points of ecstasy that no angelic lover could ever locate, or plunging me into gibbering weeping hells of pain that no torturer could ever devise."

- Moab Is My Washpot

Stephen on Being Right:

"I believe one of the greatest human failings is to prefer to be right than to be effective."

Stephen on Motivation:

"When push-off comes to shove-off, a man must have a reason to get out of bed in the mornings, something more than the threat of bedsores, at any rate."

- The Hippopotamus

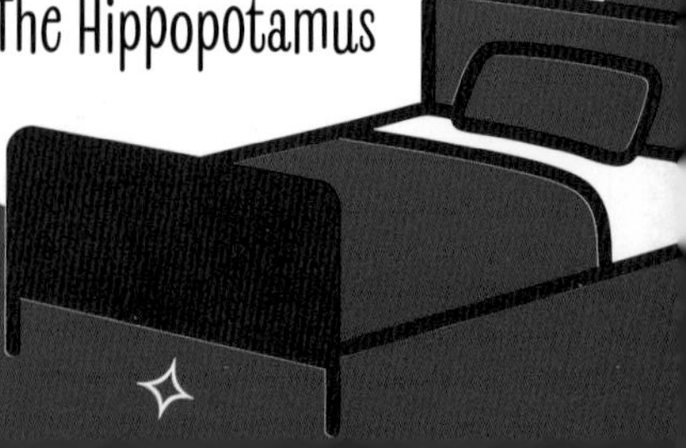

Stephen on Christmas:

"Christmas to a child is the first terrible proof that to travel hopefully is better than to arrive."

Stephen on Swearing:

"It would be impossible to imagine going through life without swearing, and without enjoying swearing."

Stephen on Men:

"Little girls grow up to be women, little boys grow up to be little boys."

- The Liar

Stephen on His Devils:

"It's not all that bad. Heightened self-consciousness, apartness, an inability to join in, physical shame, and self-loathing—they are not all bad. Those devils have also been my angels. Without them I would never have disappeared into language, literature, the mind, laughter, and all the mad intensities that made and unmade me."

- Moab Is My Washpot

Stephen on Estate Agents:

"Estate agents: like them or loathe them, you'd be mad not to loathe them."

Stephen on Cynics:

"Cynical is the name we give those we fear may be laughing at us."

- The Hippopotamus

Stephen on History:

"When the evening was over, Alistair Cooke shook my hand goodbye and held it firmly, saying, 'This hand you are shaking once shook the hand of Bertrand Russell.'

'Wow!' I said, duly impressed.

'No, No,' said Cooke, 'It goes further than that. Bertrand Russell knew Robert Browning. Bertrand Russell's aunt danced with Napoleon. That's how close we all are to history. Just a few handshakes away. Never forget that.'"

- The Fry Chronicles

Stephen on Heroes:

"Few heroes die peacefully in their beds after long lives filled with happiness."

- Heroes: Mortals and Monsters, Quests and Adventures

Stephen on Music Lovers

"There is simply no limit to the tyrannical snobbery that otherwise decent people can descend into when it comes to music."

- Moab Is My Washpot

Stephen on Peak and Decline:

"The moment when flowers and fruits are at their fullest and ripest is the moment that precedes their fall, their decay, their rot, their death."

- Troy

Stephen on Morality:

"If you spend your life on a moral hill-top, you see nothing but the mud below. If, like me, you live in the mud itself, you get a damned good view of clear blue sky and clean green hills above. There's none so evil-minded as those with a moral mission, and none so pure in heart as the depraved."

- The Hippopotamus

Stephen on Love:

"Come to think of it, I don't know that love has a point, which is what makes it so glorious. Sex has a point, in terms of relief and, sometimes, procreation, but love, like all art, as Oscar said,is quite useless."

- Moab Is My Washpot

Stephen on Destiny:

"Even meaning and destiny themselves can be read in ordinary things, if you have the gift."

- Mythos: The Greek Myths Retold

Stephen on Being Kind:

"It's enough to be benign, to be gentle, to be funny, to be kind."

Stephen on Self-Hatred:

"Counterintuitively, self-hatred is one of the leading symptoms of clinical narcissism. Only by telling yourself and the world how much you hate yourself can you receive the reliable shower of praise and admiration in response that you feel you deserve..."

- More Fool Me

Stephen on Religion:

"...Catholic versus Protestant, essentially. It's that kind of fight. ... And it goes on to this day. Will we never learn? Who knows? Religion. S*** it."

- QI, Series 4

Stephen on Being Human:

"To be human and to be adult means constantly to be in the grip of opposing emotions, to have daily to reconcile apparently conflicting tensions. I want this, but need that. I cherish this, but I adore its opposite too."

"We keep our insignificant blemishes so that we can blame them for our larger defects."

- Moab Is My Washpot

Stephen on Fame:

"How strange is our mortal zest for fame. Perhaps it is the only way humans can be gods. We achieve immortality not through ambrosia and ichor but through history and reputation. Through statues and epic song."

- Troy

"I found it all about as arousing as a Tupperware party."

- Moab Is My Washpot

Stephen on feelings:

"Feelings are not something to which one does or does not have rights."

- stephenfry.com, June 2013

Stephen on February:

"It was a Tuesday in February. Many of my life's most awful moments have taken place on Tuesdays. And what is February if not the Tuesday of the year?"

- Moab Is My Washpot

Stephen on the Existence of a God:

"You can't just say there is a god because the world is beautiful. You have to account for bone cancer in children."

Stephen on Wanting to be Liked:

"Wanting to be liked is often a very unlikeable characteristic."

- The Fry Chronicles

Stephen on English:

"The English language is an arsenal of weapons; if you are going to brandish them without checking to see whether or not they are loaded, you must expect to have them explode in your face from time to time. 'Poppycock' means 'soft s***'—from the Dutch, I need scarcely remind you, pappe kak."

- The Liar

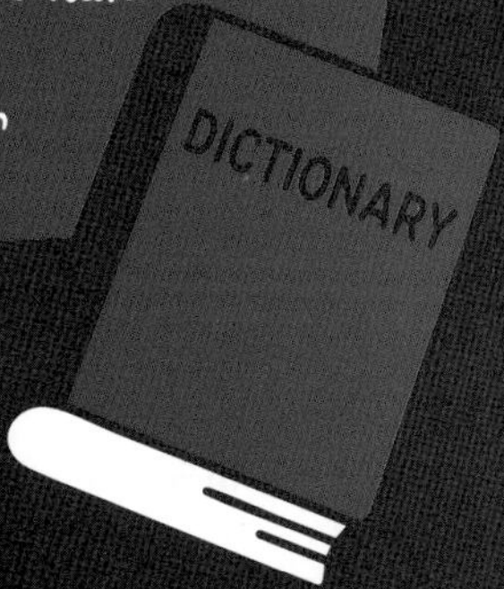

Stephen on His Mental Health:

"Nowadays, a lot of what was wrong with me would no doubt be ascribed to Attention Deficit Disorder, tartrazine food colouring, dairy produce, and air pollution. A few hundred years earlier, it would have been demons, still the best analogy I think, but not much help when it comes to a cure."

- Moab Is My Washpot

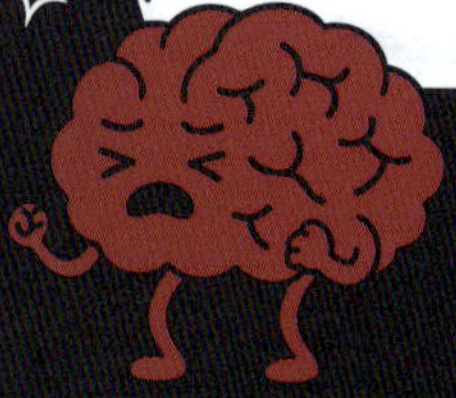

Stephen on Poetry:

"You want poetry, first you have to muck in with humanity, you have to fight with paper and pencil for weeks and weeks until your heart bleeds: verses aren't channelled into your head by angels or muses or sprites of nature."

- The Hippopotamus

Stephen on Stupidity:

"Ask a stupid person, you'll get a stupid answer."

Stephen on Convicts:

"To expect a convict to have the strength to give up smoking is to expect a leopard to change his spots, become vegetarian, and learn to knit, all on the same day."

- The Fry Chronicles

Stephen on Cosmetics:

"The trouble with doing a thing for cosmetic reasons is that one always ends up with a cosmetic result, and cosmetic results, as we know from inspecting rich American women, are ludicrous, embarrassing, and horrific."

- Moab Is My Washpot

Stephen on Writing:

"I get an urge, like a pregnant elephant, to go away and give birth to a book."

Stephen on Princess Diana:

"Princess Diana holds in the threshold for a second longer, checks over her shoulder that her Prince is out of earshot, and whispers softly in my ear, 'Sorry to leave early, though secretly I'm quite glad. It's Spitting Image tonight, and I want to watch it in my room. They hate it, of course. I absolutely adore it."

- More Fool Me

Stephen on Blame:

"Blame, certainly, is a dish only edible when served fresh and warm. Old blames, grudges, and scores congeal and curdle and cause the most terrible indigestion."

- Moab Is My Washpot

Stephen on Being Offended:

"If I had a large amount of money I should certainly found a hospital for those whose grip upon the world is so tenuous that they can be severely offended by words and phrases and yet remain all unoffended by the injustice, violence, and oppression that howls daily about our ears."

- Loose Ends, BBC Radio 4, circa 1987

Stephen on Apologies:

"It is a little theory of mine that has much exercised my mind lately, that most of the problems of this silly and delightful world derive from our apologising for those things which we ought not to apologise for, and failing to apologise for those things for which apology is necessary."

- Moab Is My Washpot

Stephen on Identity:

"We are not nouns, we are verbs. I am not a thing–an actor, a writer–I am a person who does things–I write, I act–and I never know what I'm going to do next. I think you can be imprisoned if you think of yourself as a noun."

Stephen on Education:

"Education is the sum of what students teach each other between lectures and seminars."

Stephen on Life:

"Know this: we are a long time dead. Life may be short, but it is sweet."

- Heroes: Mortals and Monsters, Quests and Adventures

Stephen on Shame:

"Just as it is the love of money that is the root of all evil, it is the belief in shamefulness that is the root of all misery."

- Moab Is My Washpot

Stephen on Playing the Piano:

"I can play… I mean, as an effort of will, I can sit down and learn a piece at the piano and reproduce it, so that those who hear will not necessarily move away with their hands clutched to their mouths, vomit leaking through fingers, blood dripping from ears."

- Moab Is My Washpot

Stephen on Swearing:

"I hate it when people say swearing isn't necessary. Things not being necessary is what makes life interesting, the little extras in life."

Stephen on Being Tone Deaf:

"I'm not even tone deaf, that's the arse-mothering, f***-nosed, b*gger-sucking w*nk of the thing.I'M NOT EVEN TONE F***ING DEAF. I'm tone DUMB."

- Moab Is My Washpot

Stephen on Self-Shame:

"Since my earliest years, I felt nothing but shame for the useless casing of flesh I inhabit."

- The Times, September 2010

Stephen on The Future:

"The future is a much bigger deal than the past."

- The Liar

Stephen on His Schooldays:

"'Late, Fry?'
'Really, sir? So am I.'
'Don't try to be clever, boy.'
'Very good, sir. How stupid would you like me to be? Very stupid or only slightly stupid?'"

- Moab Is My Washpot

Stephen on Trying:

"As Yoda had expressed it a long time ago in a galaxy far, far away: 'Do. Or do not. There is no try.'"

- Heroes: Mortals and Monsters, Quests and Adventures